Cover *Ayatollah Khomeini addresses a crowd of fervent supporters.*

Frontispiece *The Islamic army march on the anniversary of the martyrdom of Husain — the holiest day in the Shiite calendar.*

THE REVOLUTION IN IRAN

Akbar Husain

ROURKE ENTERPRISES INC.
Vero Beach, Florida 32964

Text © 1988 Rourke Enterprises Inc.
PO Box 3328, Vero Beach, Florida 32964

Manufactured in England

Library of Congress Cataloging in Publication Data
Husain, Akbar.
    The revolution in Iran/Akbar Husain.
      p.   cm.—(Flashpoints)
    British ed. published: Hove, East Sussex, England:
    Wayland, 1986.
    Bibliography: p.
    Includes index.
    Summary: Discusses the origins, events, conclusion,
and aftermath of the conflict in Iran after Ayatollah
Khomeini returned from exile to lead the 1979
revolution.
    ISBN 0-86592-038-9
    1. Iran—History—1979——Juvenile literature.
[1. Iran— History—1979–]. I. Title. II. Series:
Flashpoints (Vero Beach, Fla.)
DS318.H87   1989
955′.054—dc19   88-2453   CIP   AC

Contents

1
Return of the Ayatollah

> Every revolution was first a thought in one man's mind, and when that same thought occurs to another man, it is the key to that era.
>
> Ralph Waldo Emerson *Essays*

After his long exile, Ayatollah Khomeini returns to Iran to lead the Islamic revolution, in February 1979.

On February 1, 1979, a chartered Air France jumbo jet carried the 78-year-old Ayatollah Ruhollah Khomeini, undoubted leader of the Iranian revolution, from his exile in Paris to Tehran. Two weeks earlier, the Shah had

departed from Iran "on vacation," leaving Shahpour Bakhtiar's reformist government in charge of implementing constitutional changes intended to save the Shah's throne. By deciding to fly to Iran, Khomeini was challenging the government that had discouraged him from returning. Three million people turned out to welcome Khomeini, giving him such a tumultuous reception that his passage through the streets became impossible, requiring part of the journey to be made by helicopter.

Khomeini's first public act was to visit Behesht-e-Zahra —Tehran's sprawling cemetery—where those who had died in the previous fourteen months' struggle lay buried. There he made an emotional memorial address not only to Iranians but also to the outside world: "Is it human rights that when we want to name a government, we get instead a cemetery full of people?"

Declaring Bakhtiar and his government illegal as they derived their power from the Shah, Khomeini named Mehdi Bazargan as prime minister of the revolutionary government. Iran was thus in the peculiar position of having two rival governments. Within days, the machinery of government as well as the military drifted toward Khomeini, leaving Prime Minister Bakhtiar exposed and powerless—a leader without a following.

Surrounded by friends and well-wishers, Shah Reza Pahlavi, with Queen Farah behind him, prepares to leave Iran, never to return.

9

Map showing Iran's position in the Middle East.

On Sunday, February 11, after several days of skirmishes between revolutionaries and loyalists, Tehran Radio announced the final victory of the revolution with the words: "This is the voice of Tehran, the voice of true Iran, the voice of revolution. The dictatorship has come to an end."

In time, the Iranian revolution will take its place among the great revolutionary movements that have swept through the United States, France, the Soviet Union and China, changing in their wake the course of history. But although the Iranian revolution has common economic and social causes with many of these other revolutions, its religious character makes it unique.

2
Religious roots

Verily, God changes not what is in a people, until they change what is in themselves.

The Koran

In order to understand the phenomenon of Khomeini and the religious zeal of his followers, it is necessary to examine the roots of Shiism, one of the two main branches of Islam (the other being Sunnism) and the established form of religion in Iran. The Shiite branch traces its roots to a split that occurred at the death of the Prophet Muhammad. According to Shiite tradition, Muhammad nominated Ali, his son-in-law and favored confidant, to succeed him as Caliph (the spiritual and civil ruler). However, on the Prophet's death, one of his comrades, Abu Bakr, was elected instead to the Caliphate. The split between Shiites and Sunnis hinges on this succession. While Shiites supported the candidacy of Ali, Sunnis maintained the legitimacy of the election of Abu Bakr, according to the Arab tradition of electoral procedure.

The religious nature of the Iranian revolution singles it out from other revolutions.

Ali, who was then thirty-three years old, did not challenge Abu Bakr's succession, as he wished to maintain the unity of the newly emergent Islam. Over the next twenty-five years three Caliphs were elected, and on the assassination of the third, the elders of Medina asked Ali to take over the Caliphate in an effort to ease the disarray in the Muslim Commonwealth.

Ali ruled for five years before being assassinated. On his death, Muawiyah, the governor of Syria, proclaimed himself Caliph, again denying the rights of Ali's family. During Muawiyah's twenty-year rule, Ali's sons Hassan and Husain shunned politics, dedicating themselves to religious works. However, when Muawiyah's son Yezid became Caliph, two events coincided to end the uneasy truce between the Prophet's family (represented by Husain) and the rulers. First, Yezid demanded that Husain swear the oath of allegiance to him—something that Muawiyah had diplomatically avoided. Second, the citizens of Kufa, a city in Iraq, asked Husain to help them get rid of the tyrannical governor appointed by Yezid.

On the way to Kufa, Husain was cut off by Yezid's armies at Kerbala desert. Husain's small band of 72 men faced Yezid's 4,000-strong force. On the tenth day of Muharram (the first month in the Muslim calendar) A.D. 680, after a bloody battle, all but two of Husain's party were killed. This epic battle is annually commemorated by Shiites, as

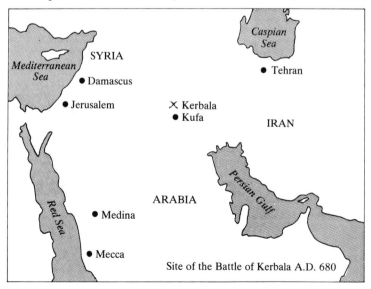

Map showing the site of the battle of Kerbala, which is annually commemorated by Shiite Muslims.

The muezzin, who calls Muslims to prayer five times a day.

not only did it symbolize to them the struggle between good and evil but it also underlined Husain's defiance of an unjust authority—a belief that lies embedded at the heart of Shiism. His was a challenge to an oppressive ruler who had seized the Caliphate and had violated basic human rights, and who had also intended to strike at the foundations of Islam by destroying the Prophet's family.

In modern-day Iran similar chords were struck when the Shah was seen as Yezid while Khomeini represented Husain's challenge to a corrupt, autocratic establishment. Considering the turbulent birth of Shiism it is not surprising that religion and politics are closely interwoven in Iran, where Shiism has been the state religion since 1501.

In Islam, no formal priesthood was originally intended because people can have direct communion with God. However, a type of clergy did develop to guide the spiritually unlearned. The ulema, as they were called, gained authority from their role as judges in the interpretation of Shariah (Islamic) Law, and as teachers, providing the only education available until the twentieth century. The ulema also played an important social role in drawing together the various strands of society under the umbrella of religion. In addition, they had economic power because of the large religious contributions that were given to them.

Socially powerful and economically independent, the ulema were largely invulnerable to secular pressures and, therefore, provided an effective counterweight to the power of the state.

13

3
Historical roots

Revolutions are not made. They come. A revolution is as natural a growth as an oak. It comes out of the past. Its foundations are laid back in history.

Wendell Phillips
Speech at Boston to the Anti-Slavery Society, 1852

The constitutional revolution
The Qajars were the ruling dynasty in Iran from 1785. Until 1906, the king (called the Shah) ruled as absolute monarch, retaining total control over legislative, executive and judicial functions, and delegating only nominal powers to the minister. The Qajars introduced many Westernizing reforms dur-

The Qajar Shah Mohammed Ali, who was forced to abdicate in 1909 after an uprising in Tabriz.

*The Shah's young son
Ahmad, who took the
throne when his father
abdicated.*

ing the nineteenth century. The ulema felt threatened by some of these reforms, which undercut their authority. They resented the selling of concessions, the increasing secularization and the growing dominance of Russian and British interests in Iranian affairs, so they exerted pressure to try to halt the tide of change.

To finance their extravagant lifestyle the Qajars periodically sold concessions to foreigners. In this respect, the 1872 concession won by Baron Julius de Reuter deserves special mention. The concession sold to Reuter gave him exclusive rights, for twenty-five years, to exploit all the existing and potential economic resources of Iran, including railroads, mines and banks. Even Lord Curzon, a firm colonialist, called it "the most complete and extraordinary surrender of the entire industrial resources of a kingdom into foreign hands that had probably been dreamed of." Russian protests and a widespread public outcry led by the ulema forced the state to back down and cancel the concession.

Reza Khan, who abolished the Qajar dynasty and appointed himself Shah in 1926, thus founding the Pahlavi dynasty.

Opposition mounted, and in 1906 widespread protests forced the Shah to grant a constitution and establish a *majlis*, a form of parliament, diminishing his role to that of a ruler in name only. The aim of this constitution was to ensure the compatibility of the law of the land with that of Islam, calling for a special committee that would only approve legislation in line with Shiite doctrine. This constitution was short-lived, though, because the Russians, who were concerned about the curbs placed on the powers of the Shah, helped the Shah to dissolve the constitution.

In 1909 the people of Tabriz rose up against the Shah, calling for the establishment of a second majlis. The Shah was seen as the puppet of the Russians, who were viewed with great suspicion by the Iranians because of their slow and steady advance into Iranian territory. The Shah had to abdicate and leave the country, appointing his son Ahmad as his successor.

By 1911, the constitutional revolution was at an end. As a result of internal problems and under pressure from the Russians, the government dissolved the majlis.

During World War I both Russia and Britain occupied Iran. The British supported the rise of Reza Khan, the commander of the Northern Cossack Brigade. They were alarmed at the weakness of the Qajar Shah, the influence of now-communist Russia (since the 1917 Bolshevik revolution), and they wished to gain access to Iraq, which was then occupied by Germany's allies the Turks. They saw Reza Khan as a natural successor to the weakening Shah.

In 1921 Reza Khan marched on Tehran, imposed martial law, and appointed a puppet prime minister. By 1923, having consolidated his power, he named himself prime minister. The majlis, in the absence of the Qajar Shah who had fled from Iran, abolished the Qajar dynasty and in 1925 voted for a transfer of title of Shah to the prime minister. Reza Khan thereby founded the Pahlavi dynasty.

Reza Shah—founder of the Pahlavi dynasty

Reza Khan crowned himself Shah on April 26, 1926, taking the name of his dynasty, Pahlavi, from the language of pre-Islamic Iran.

One of Reza Shah's policies of Westernization was the abolition of the chadur, *or veil, that Islamic women have always worn. This upset the religious classes.*

17

Impressed by the Westernization of neighboring Turkey under Mustafa Kemal Ataturk, Reza Shah introduced measures to secure his absolute rule as well as the formation of a secular state. To accomplish this it was necessary for him to destroy traditional centers of power. He eliminated the tribal chiefs, canceled aristocratic titles and honors, subordinated the power of the judiciary and neutralized the authority of the majlis. It remained for him to tame the ulema.

Between 1925 and 1930, new commercial, civil and criminal codes were introduced, thereby curtailing the judicial power of the ulema. Western dress was introduced and women were unveiled by decree, so they no longer had to wear the *chadur* (the long black cloak covering all but the face); gatherings to commemorate Husain's martyrdom during Muharram were banned; religious endowments and charitable trusts were confiscated; and religious leaders were forcibly or subtly co-opted into acquiescence with the Shah's desires. By 1941 the ulema, in the face of a unified military and strong central authority, found their influence greatly undermined.

Mohammad Reza Shah

In 1941, Reza Shah was forced to abdicate by the occupying Allies (Britain and Russia) because of his Nazi sympathies. His son, Mohammad Reza, who was only twenty-one, acceded to the throne, and played a minor role while the Allies occupied Iran and power was passed on to the hitherto impotent majlis deputies.

During World War II, Iran was of strategic importance to the Allies. In 1942 the British needed a course of retreat from North Africa in the face of Rommel's offensive. Iranian oil was critical for fueling the armies' vehicles. By 1942 the Russians had entered the war and required arms and supplies. They found that the supply route through the Baltic was hazardous, incurring heavy losses, so the establishment of a route from the Persian Gulf to the Caucasus through Iran was vital for the transportation of these supplies. The strategic importance of Iran resulted in Russia's occupying the north, and Britain the south.

By 1946, however, a new war had begun—the Cold War. The communist Tudeh Party of Iran, with Russian backing, attempted to form an autonomous state in northern Iran, but was halted by U.S. intervention. The United States

was eager to thwart Soviet influence and also to stake its own claim on Iran's valuable oil resources.

Rise and fall of Mossadegh

By 1950, although the Shah had begun to consolidate his power, the demand for nationalization of the oil industry swept the country and became interlinked with the cause of sovereignty. It was felt that the influence of the Anglo-Iranian oil company was too dominant, with claims that members of the majlis were in the pay of the company, and that if Iran was to benefit economically from its natural resource, a revision of the agreement between the two countries was essential.

Shah Mohammad Reza (left) with members of the Muslim hierarchy, who were suspicious of his attempts to curb their power.

The body of Prime Minister Ali Razmara, who was assassinated in 1951 by a member of an Islamic sect.

The challenge to the government on these issues was led by a seventy-year-old aristocrat and leader of the National Front Party, Dr. Mohammad Mossadegh. Mossadegh's policies of oil nationalization, true democracy and freedom from interference by external powers galvanized the public along with the bazaaris and ulema, and gave him a virtually impregnable position.

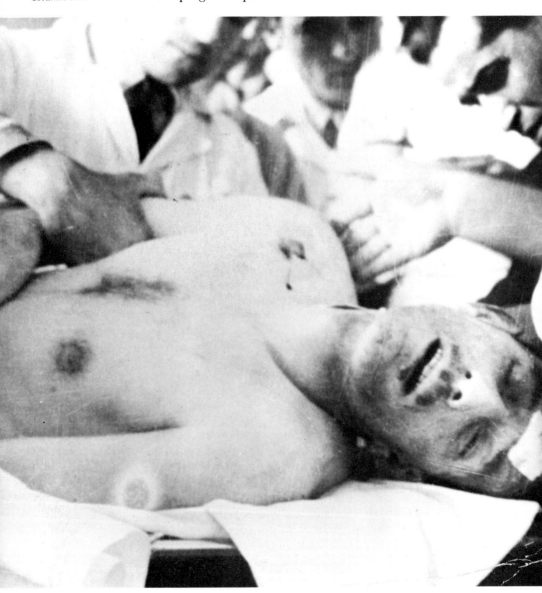

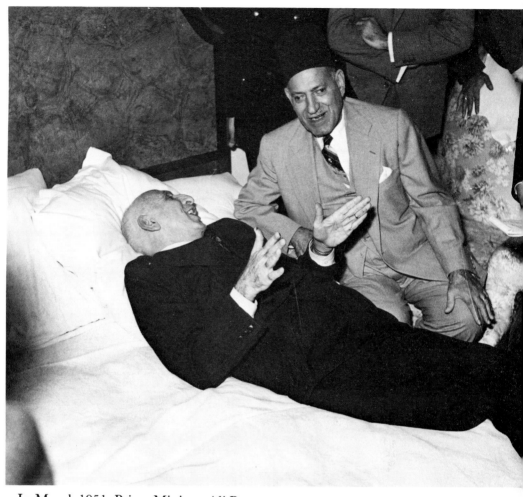

In March 1951, Prime Minister Ali Razmara was assassinated, and in the resulting chaos, the Oil Nationalization Bill raced through parliament and an unprepared Mossadegh was swept to power as prime minister. For the next two years, Mossadegh governed a country and an economy under seige. The major oil companies (led by the exclusive shareholder—British Petroleum) boycotted the purchase of Iranian oil, and conservative agents supported by the Shah and foreign powers stirred up economic and political chaos. Although the Tudeh Party revived its network of underground cells, it also opposed Mossadegh at every turn, believing that it would be the natural successor if the government was brought down.

Prime Minister Mossadegh giving an interview from his bed, while on a trip to Egypt in 1951.

21

On August 16, 1953 an attempt was made by royalist forces to reinstate the Shah. It was unsuccessful, and the Shah fled the country. He returned three days later when a coup organized by the CIA (Central Intelligence Agency) succeeded in toppling Mossadegh, thereby extinguishing the last flicker of hope for the establishment of a genuine democracy.

Oil was denationalized and the British monopoly broken. Britain retained a 40 percent share, while the Americans gained 40 percent. The balance of 20 percent went to Dutch–French interests. Not only was British control weakened on the economic stage but the Americans also became the senior political partners.

Tanks patrolling in Tehran's main square following the coup that overthrew Mossadegh and reinstated the Shah in 1953.

A citizen who has benefited from the land reform program throws himself at the feet of the Shah in thanks.

The White Revolution

The Shah set about strengthening his power, using the security agency SAVAK (organized with Israeli and U.S. assistance), which was established in 1953 to keep strict control. The opposition were rendered ineffective and an uneasy truce lasted until 1961 when President Kennedy of the United States encouraged the Shah toward greater liberalization. The Shah reacted in 1962 by proclaiming the White Revolution—so called because it was to be a social and economic revolution without bloodshed. It comprised a six-point program that included land reform, giving the vote to women, and changes in electoral law to enable non-Muslims to stand as candidates. The ulema were unhappy with the land reform program, which would take away their entitlement to religious endowments of property (known as *waqfs*). Changes in the electoral law were taken by them as direct assaults on Islam.

Until 1962, the ulema were content to engage in their religious pursuits, cowed by the overwhelming power of the state. However, this was soon to change as a fiery religious leader threw down the gauntlet. Ayatollah Ruhollah Khomeini began by roundly denouncing the Shah, and his partnership with the United States and Israel, and then he

The Shah and Queen Farah arriving at the opening of the Iranian parliament. It was the first time a woman had attended an opening in the history of the country.

Ayatollah Ruhollah Khomeini, who burst on to the political scene in 1963.

criticized widespread corruption, particularly of Islamic beliefs. In January 1963, the Shah entered Qom, the seat of theological studies in Iran, at the head of his 700-strong detachment of bodyguards, whom he had dressed as mullahs. He then made a speech denouncing the Islamic leaders as "black reactionaries" and accusing them of being "sodomites and agents of the British."

Khomeini rallied the ulema to his radical banner and counter-attacked in June 1963, on the eve of the martyrdom of Husain, thereby drawing a parallel between the government and the tyrannical Yezid. Demonstrations that followed were quickly crushed by the government's forces. Martial law was declared and leading radical ulema, including Khomeini, were arrested.

By August, political pressures had forced the Shah to release Khomeini. Throughout 1964, Khomeini enhanced his standing as a radical leader, building a strong base of support among young militants who were disillusioned with traditional secular opposition groups.

In late 1964, the government passed legislation that granted U.S. military forces in Iran immunity from Iranian law, thus preventing courts from hearing complaints against the foreigners. This was the spark to the tinder, and Khomeini strongly denounced the act:

> They have reduced the Iranian people to a level lower than that of an American dog. If someone runs over a dog belonging to an American, he will be prosecuted. Even if the Shah himself were to run over a dog belonging to an American, he would be prosecuted. But if an American cook runs over the Shah, the head of state, no one will have the right to interfere with him. Why? Because they wanted a [$200 million] loan and America demanded this in return.

The government had had enough of Khomeini and sent him into exile in Turkey, where the secular society made him feel totally alienated. His application to settle in Najaf in Iraq, the major center of Shiite learning, met with no opposition. The Iraqi ambassador in Iran commented that "There are so many mullahs in Najaf that one more or less would make no difference."

Martial law was imposed in Tehran following anti-government rioting that broke out after Khomeini's arrest.

4
Revolution!

Repression is the seed of revolution.

Daniel Webster 1845

The oil bonanza

In December 1973, the Organization of Petroleum Exporting Countries (OPEC) forced oil prices to increase. Iranian oil income rose from $4 billion in 1973 to $20 billion in 1974. Within three years, however, the bitter social and economic fruits of the boom were being harvested. There was general discontent among widespread sections of the population, including the poor, the religious conservatives, the merchants and the intelligentsia; all of whom had reasons for wanting change (see Chapter 5).

In the United States, during the 1976 election campaign, Jimmy Carter stressed that the United States would not tolerate human rights abuses from its allies, and would encourage these governments to liberalize their policies. Once in office in January 1977, Carter emphasized that human rights were an integral part of his foreign policy and indicated that those countries that were in clear violation would be denied American aid.

The Shah (right) leans over to get advice from his oil minister, Dr. Jamshid Amouzegar, at an OPEC meeting in 1975.

President Carter and his wife wipe their eyes as tear gas, intended to disperse anti-Shah demonstrators, drifts onto the White House lawns, during the welcoming ceremonies for the Shah.

Pre-revolutionary environment

Since the Shah felt secure of his domestic standing, he set about attempting to improve his international standing, seeking particularly to appease the United States. In February 1977, he began the process of liberalization, freeing 357 political prisoners. The movement began to develop its own momentum as the legal profession fired the first shots by writing a series of open letters critical of government policies, and calling for freedom of speech and free elections. This was followed by demands from the Writers' Association, the bazaar guilds and the remnants of the various political parties. In August 1977, the Shah decided to go further, responding to external pressures, to the social reawakening and to the economic malaise. He did this by replacing the prime minister and by trying to deflate the economy. His reforms did not go far enough and another opportunity to make meaningful changes was lost.

In November 1977, when the Shah visited President Carter in Washington D.C., the police dispersed anti-Shah protesters with tear gas. At the welcoming ceremonies, both leaders were in tears, as the gas drifted onto the White House lawn. The Shah then hosted a dinner for President Carter in Tehran, where the President declared: "Iran is an oasis of stability in a sea of trouble, and I am sure that the reason for this is the just, the great, the inspired leadership of your Majesty." President Carter could not have been more wrong. Under the tranquil surface, forces were converging toward revolution.

Countdown to revolution

The government lit the fuse in January 1978 when it had an article published in Tehran's daily paper *Eta'laat* slandering Khomeini, accusing him of corruption, homosexuality and reactionary politics. Publication of the article led to widespread demonstrations, sit-ins and marches to which the government reacted by sending troops to quell demonstrations with orders to shoot.

The first riots broke out in Tehran after the government published an article slandering Khomeini.

29

Revolutionary guards outside the home of Ayatollah Shariatmadari in Qom.

However, by February, demonstrations that had begun in Tehran and Qom spread to other cities. The cycle of violence intensified as demonstrations were called for by the ulema for the ritual memorials held on the fortieth day of mourning. They were to include a limited strike and general demonstrations. The army was called into Tabriz, a major provincial city, to quell disturbances that left up to 100 people dead. By the fortieth day after the Tabriz marches, protests had spread to thirty-five cities, leaving 250 people dead.

On previous occasions, use of force by the government had broken up the demonstrations. On this occasion repression revealed a rich mine of anti-government feeling, which spread swiftly throughout the country.

In Qom, Ayatollah Shariatmadari, a leading Islamic leader, called for a general strike on June 17. It was successful and passed without violence. Use of the strike weapon become more widespread as workers demonstrated for better wages and free unions.

On August 19, 400 patrons of Tehran's Rex Cinema were burned alive in a fire. The exits of the cinema were locked and the local fire department took a long time to reach the scene. The government blamed dissidents for the outrage, but the public universally believed it was committed by SAVAK.

As demonstrations gained momentum, the economy floundered and the government's ability to respond was stretched to the limit. A new approach was needed, so the Shah replaced Prime Minister Amouzegar with Jafaar Sherif Emami—a politician without scruples or credibility, but who supposedly had good links with the religious classes.

Emami published a political program to "create reconciliation among all classes" by releasing political prisoners, increasing government salaries, providing for legitimate political parties and fresh elections, waging a campaign against corruption and respecting human rights. It was an agenda that promised something for everyone, but not many people were convinced.

On Friday, September 8, a day that became known as Black Friday, government troops opened fire on unarmed demonstrators, killing and wounding many people.

31

Although Khomeini was still in exile in Iraq, he continued to send his taped messages to an ever-increasing number of supporters, exhorting them to challenge the government and demand the removal of the Pahlavi family.

On September 7, an estimated 100,000 people marched in Tehran calling for Khomeini's return, as well as the deportation of the Shah and the establishment of an Islamic republic. The government reacted by declaring martial law.

On Friday, September 8, demonstrators, some in ignorance and others in defiance of the martial law order, gathered in Zhaleh Square near the parliament buildings. Troops opened fire, and tanks and helicopter gunships were used. Black Friday, as this day was to become known, was a watershed in the revolutionary calendar. With the blatant use of armed force, the government had sown the seeds of rebellion, driving even moderate supporters into the arms of the revolution. Marchers took to wearing white burial shrouds, symbolically inviting martyrdom with its promise of a certain place in heaven. For the people, their struggle had taken on the epic proportions of Husain's challenge to Yezid's tyrannical government.

Ayatollah Khomeini leading prayers at his home near Paris, during his exile there.

The government made more symbolic changes: Hoveiyda resigned as Court Minister, various officials were charged with corruption and the royal family agreed to have no role in government.

Khomeini's emotionally charged messages sent on cassette tapes further fueled the situation. After the September 8 massacre, Khomeini declared: "Fire again. It is your brothers and sisters who will receive your bullets, but they will be praying for your forgiveness." Again, the refrain of martyrdom.

Abol Hasan Bani-Sadr who invited Khomeini to Paris and helped with the revolutionary campaign.

Khomeini flies to Paris

The tide was flowing inexorably toward revolutionary change when the Iranian government persuaded Iraq to expel Khomeini. He traveled to Paris on October 6, invited by the active Iranian Student Committee led by Abol Hasan Bani-Sadr (the first president of post-revolutionary Iran). Khomeini settled in a village 25 miles outside Paris from where he continued his revolutionary campaign. This he conducted under the gaze of the international media, which he used skillfully, giving four interviews a day.

On October 18, oil workers went on strike, cutting off the country's economic lifeline. Demonstrations continued, broadening in scope and increasing in intensity. On

November 5, demonstrators attacked banks, cinemas, air-line offices and even a section of the British Embassy—all symbols of Western domination.

After consultations with the U.S., on November 6, the Shah replaced Sherif Emami with a military government headed by General Gholam Ali-Azhari—the Commander of the Imperial Guard. The government had two objectives: to quell the disturbances and to resume oil production.

As politicians were re-arrested and strike leaders intimidated, oil production rose again. However, disturbances continued and foreigners were now threatened with violence. The government tried first conciliation and then repression. Neither worked and strike activity resumed. On November 27, the Central Bank published a list naming 177 people who had among them sent $2 billion abroad in recent weeks. The list included members of the royal family and read like the *Who's Who?* of Iran. The scale of the plunder angered many of the poorer sections of society.

Demonstrations intensified during the first week of December and culminated in massive marches on the tenth and eleventh of Muharram (days traditionally set aside to commemorate the martyrdom of Husain). As troops were withdrawn from the streets, demonstrations became peaceful.

However, it was by then evident that the military government had failed in its objectives to halt demonstrations and resume oil production. Foreigners were being scared away and the economy was spluttering to a halt. As the lack of discipline affected large portions of the army, the government began to lose control. General Azhari resigned and was replaced by a new civilian prime minister—Shahpour Bakhtiar, who took office as a follower of the nationalist ideology of Mossadegh. On January 13, Bakhtiar announced a Regency Council to take the place of the Shah while he went on "vacation." Khomeini responded by naming a provincial Islamic Revolutionary Council.

Mehdi Bazargan, whom Khomeini appointed as prime minister of the provisional Islamic government on February 5, 1979.

The final curtain

The Shah left Iran on January 16, 1979, and the country was ecstatic. Despite this substantial victory, Khomeini, who was not interested in half measures, declared Bakhtiar's government illegitimate as it derived its power from the Shah. Demonstrations continued, and while they were not blatantly anti-Bakhtiar, the cycle of violence was breaking out anew. Khomeini announced his intention to return to

Opposite *Military officers, mullahs and ministers line up for prayers at Tehran University, led by Sayed Ali Khamenei.*

35

Shahpour Bakhtiar announcing that he will not resign, despite Khomeini's demands for him to do so.

Iran on January 26, and Bakhtiar responded by closing the airports, playing for time. Three days later when air force technicians overran Tehran airport, Bakhtiar was forced to reopen it. Khomeini arrived to a conqueror's reception. As the revolutionary leader arrived to lead the people, the 400,000-strong royalist army stood in the wings, ready to thwart his ambitions. Although Bakhtiar was still prime minister, on February 5, Khomeini appointed Mehdi Bazargan as prime minister of the provisional Islamic government. Members of the armed forces began to defect to Khomeini's side.

On February 11, revolutionaries and deserters overran military bases and began distributing weapons. The Imperial Guard attempted to stop them but were easily crushed. General Gharabaghi—Chairman of the Military Supreme Council—ordered the troops back to barracks. By this time, however, it was an empty gesture as there were no troops at his command. Bakhtiar fled the country. On February 12, Prime Minister Mehdi Bazargan inaugurated the Islamic government of Iran by presenting his cabinet to Khomeini.

5
Causes of the revolution

A great revolution is never the fault of the people but of the government.

Goethe

The Shah ultimately lost his throne because his policies had alienated nearly all sectors of society, including the emerging middle class, the bazaaris, the peasants, the urban working classes and the ulema.

The middle class felt intellectually and politically stifled in the restrictive climate dictated by the Shah. Although

The bazaar, the traditional marketplace of Iran.

The wealth arising from the oil boom did not filter down to the 40 percent of the population who lived in conditions of appalling poverty.

they participated in the oil boom by obtaining inflated salaries, they nursed a grudge against the foreigners who earned even more and monopolized the key decision-making roles. They were attracted by Khomeini's simple chauvinism.

The conservative, religious bazaaris were traditional opponents of the Shah's dictatorship. To weaken their hold

on the economy, the government established state purchasing corporations for wheat, meat and sugar. Supermarkets that competed with the bazaar were offered subsidized credit. To undermine the social fabric of the bazaar, the government used town planning and road building as an excuse to destroy sections of the bazaars. Naturally, the bazaar

The Shah opens a water-filtering station in Tehran, one step toward bringing Iran into the twentieth century.

merchants supported the only credible opposition to the government—Khomeini and the ulema.

The economic miracle did not touch the lives of the masses (40 percent of the population) who lived at or below subsistence level in the towns and villages. Rather they were socially, culturally and economically alienated from the wealthy government and were driven into the arms of a charity-dispensing ulema.

Even the entrepreneurs and upper classes, who were the prime beneficiaries of the Shah's economic policies, sent over $10 billion of their capital overseas, betraying the system that had provided them with spectacular profits.

The ulema had the most to lose in the materialistic, Western-orientated society that the Shah had decreed. Although their central role as educators and judges had been reduced, they used the network of mosques to gather together the discontented. The ulema were ready to exploit the economic, political, social, cultural and religious causes that converged to provide revolutionary change.

Economic causes

As a result of the 1973 oil price increases, Iran's oil revenues rose fivefold to $20 billion in 1974. This encouraged the government to embark on a wildly ambitious $70-billion Development Plan for the five-year period beginning in 1973. The Plan created unrealistically high expectations: the military were to get more weapons; industrialists would get better technology and foreign expertise; the man in the street would be provided with low-cost housing, education, food subsidies and jobs; everybody would be happy in a utopian society based on oil wealth.

The Shah airily dismissed the caution of technocrats who did not fully share his vision of Iran's becoming the world's fifth industrial power by the end of the century. He set unrealistic targets, and the results were raw material shortages, lack of skilled workers and fierce inflation.

The shortage of a skilled, professional local workforce resulted in the recruitment of foreigners who were often paid many times more than Iranians doing the same job. This further fueled inflation while at the same time superimposing an alien culture onto the still traditional society.

By 1975, inflation was running at 40 percent per year. The objective of the revised Fifth Plan (1974–78) to increase the income of the poor was in jeopardy as the gap between them and the rich sections of society widened. The Shah reacted by encouraging companies to sell 49 percent of their shares to the public and employees, and also instituted a price-control program. As workers had no money to buy shares, shares ended up with speculators and in government trusts.

By 1975, as industrialized countries were in the grip of severe recession brought about by oil price increases, demand for oil decreased, resulting in reduced revenues (down to $19 billion in 1976). In spite of this, the Shah encouraged discounted deals and oil barter arrangements, adamantly maintaining the spending programs that

Resentment was felt toward the foreign workers in the oil industry, who were often paid many times more than their Iranian counterparts.

included a massive defense budget.

The decline in agriculture coupled with the lure of jobs in the towns led to a migration of 250,000 people per year from the villages. The Shah's desire for Iran to become a major Middle Eastern power was encouraged by the United States, which saw Iran as a crucial ally on the turbulent Middle East stage. Accordingly, the U.S. supplied all the military equipment requested by the Shah—at appropriately inflated prices. Iranian military expenditure soared from $1 billion in 1973 to $4.5 billion in 1974 and amounted to $30 billion for the five-year period until 1978.

Corruption on a massive scale became an accepted form of business dealing. The royal family provided for themselves by having shares in every major industrial enterprise and a percentage of total oil revenues.

The recession resulted in widespread disaffection, a belief that the oil wealth had been pillaged by a select few and heightened antipathy toward the large group (70,000 or so) of foreigners who were seen as the new colonialists.

Political causes

When the Shah eliminated Mossadegh, he neutralized the only politician who dared to pose a threat to him. After 1953, the Shah ruled Iran absolutely, supported by a powerful security force (SAVAK), while maintaining a semblance

Shad-Azfa, a SAVAK secret police officer, being tried for allegedly torturing large numbers of political prisoners.

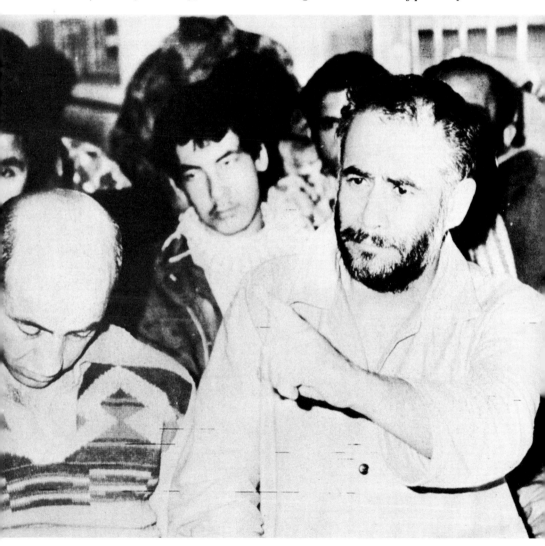

of two-party democracy. In March 1975, he dispensed with even this pretence, replacing the two parties with a single loyalist party—Rastakhiz (Resurgence). With this retrogressive step, he alienated the liberals, who were the main beneficiaries of the oil wealth, and who saw little hope of intellectual or political growth in such an environment. The Shah ruled by allowing his ministers and even prime minister no significant decision-making powers. Consequently, ministers implemented only weak and defensive policies, designed to ensure their survival, shunning any initiatives that may have carried risks.

The Shah's method of government was intended to preserve his personal power, but it left him dangerously exposed when the political house of cards began to collapse. The Shah looked for scapegoats and acknowledged the excesses of the regime in the latter stages of the revolutionary movement, but this belated recognition of the problem lacked credibility, and by this time the movement had developed a momentum of its own.

The Shah's twin foreign policies of public support for Israel, which was not recognized by most other Muslim countries, and staunch pro-Americanism, were diametrically opposed to popular feeling. As grievances against increasing foreign domination and the large numbers of U.S. military personnel based in Iran grew, the Shah was caricatured as an American puppet. This theme conveniently elevated Khomeini into an authentic Iranian patriot.

Opposite *The Shah aimed to bring primary education to the villages, where many schools did not even own a blackboard.*

Social and cultural causes

The oil wealth brought to the cities a flood of imported culture that threatened to swamp traditional Iranian cultural and social values. Nightclubs, dance halls, cinemas and bars sprang up, serving not only the large immigrant population but also the local wealthy classes.

With their bikini-clad women, the Caspian beaches resembled those of the southern Mediterranean more than those of a Muslim country. Increasing numbers of foreigners in administration and management roles created tremendous resentment among educated Iranians. The royal family's alienation from popular opinion was so pronounced that the Queen became patron of the Annual Arts Festival, which showed Western *avant garde* and X-rated films.

As a result of the unsuccessful agricultural policy, there

was mass migration to the towns, which worsened the already bad situation in housing, health and education.

Religious causes

Iran is a fundamentally religious society. In 1978, there were 180,000 ulema (that is, 1 for every 200 population) who could communicate directly with the masses through the network of mosques and the sermons given traditionally on Fridays, usually with political as well as religious messages. The challenge to the government issued by Khomeini in 1963 inspired the younger ulema. They were angered by growing materialism and the gradual destruction of traditional and religious values.

The ulema saw their works and power under threat from a liberal, Western-orientated, anti-clerical government. At just this point, they were urged by Khomeini to challenge the government. Gathering together the dispossessed, the bazaaris, the intelligentsia and the leftists under their banner, they were catapulted into revolutionary action.

Opposite *The opulence of palace life was in stark contrast to the poverty in the towns and villages.*

Below *The Shah visits religious leaders in Mash-Had, who were angered by his policies of Westernization.*

6
Aftermath

There was reason to fear that like Saturn, the Revolution might devour each of its children in turn . . .

Pierre Vigniaud *Histoire des Girondins*

During the revolutionary struggle, all major opposition groups, ranging from religious to communist, set aside their differences, united in their purpose to overthrow the Shah's regime. Inevitably, on the collapse of the old order, this fragile unity cracked, revealing natural rivalries and distinctly differing visions of post-revolutionary Iran.

The ulema supported Khomeini's vision of an Islamic government to be led by them. Their natural followers were

After the revolution the Shah's portrait on bank bills was replaced with a picture of the Iranian people.

the peasants, the urban working classes and the religious bazaaris who had financed the revolution. Liberal ulema and religious laymen did not support an Islamic system, but they did defer to the ulema for resolution of thorny issues of morality or law. Secular political parties, led by the National Front, were supported by the Western-orientated intelligentsia. The Mujahedeen-e-Khalq Party led the young and militant toward their vision of an egalitarian Marxist state wrapped in Islam. The Tudeh and the Fedayeen-e-Khalq parties saw the revolution as a means to attain a socialist utopia.

The curtain rises

The collapse of the *ancien régime* was followed by a period in which the public government was shadowed by a secret revolutionary section made up primarily of the religious leaders. Bazargan complained publicly that he was "a knife without a blade." Secret courts ordered the execution of hundreds of officials of the Shah's regime, and later executions included dissidents, social misfits and sexual deviants. Bazargan denounced the executions over which he had no control as "irreligious, inhuman and a disgrace to the country and the revolution." Liberal ulema, too, disassociated themselves from the state-sponsored terror.

Government and constitution

On March 30, 1979, a referendum was held to decide on the form of the government. The choices were stark. A vote for an Islamic republic was on a green ballot (the color of Islam), while a vote against was on a red ballot (the color of Yezid).

Despite a left-wing boycott, the result was a foregone conclusion. On April 1, Khomeini declared an Islamic republic. The 1905 constitution was amended, reverting to an Islamic model by creating a supreme position of *valayate-faqih* (rule of the jurist) for Khomeini. This supreme leader was given sweeping dictatorial powers including the selection of the president and authority over the executive, legislative and judicial branches of state power.

While these administrative matters were being handled, a fierce debate raged on through the summer regarding relations with the United States. Although anti-American feelings ran high, Prime Minister Bazargan believed he had the support of the powerful shadow cabinet, the Revolutionary Council, to pursue talks with the U.S. On November 1, 1979, Bazargan met Brzezinski, the American National Security Adviser, in Algiers. A week earlier, the Shah had been allowed to enter the U.S. on medical grounds as it was revealed he was suffering from cancer.

The collapse of the old order was followed by a period of terror, with hundreds of executions following summary Islamic trials.

The second revolution

On November 4, 1979, the American Embassy in Tehran was overrun by 400 revolutionary youths who took fifty-two of the embassy staff hostage. Although Khomeini may not have known about the plan in advance, he promptly gave

it his blessing. On November 6, Bazargan, publicly humiliated by his failure to free the hostages, handed in his resignation. With the fall of Bazargan, the hope of liberal religious democracy was lost. The first presidential elections under the new constitution were held in January 1980. Bani-Sadr, Khomeini's confidant since his exile in Paris, was the favored choice. As Khomeini decreed that religious leaders could not stand for the presidency, Ayatollah Beheshti (who had founded the Islamic Republic Party in 1979) was disqualified from running. Consequently, Bani-Sadr became the republic's first president.

By the time parliamentary elections were held in March and May the Islamic Republic Party (IRP) and its allies were well prepared, gaining a clear majority with 130 seats in the 220-member majlis. Talks between the United States and Iran on the hostages went nowhere because of domestic political maneuvering. On April 25, 1980, in desperation, the U.S. launched a military mission to free the hostages, which turned out to be a monumental failure. Of the eight helicopters and six C-130 transport planes used in the mission, three helicopters suffered severe damage and a fourth collided with a C-130, killing eight American servicemen.

An armed Islamic revolutionary stands guard in a polling station, where the referendum on the Islamic republic is taking place.

In July 1979, with the IRP-dominated majlis in formal session, the provisional Islamic Revolutionary Council was dissolved. President Bani-Sadr was forced to accept the IRP candidate, Mohamed Ali Rajai, as prime minister.

The abortive American rescue mission caused widespread suspicion of coups, real and imagined. Bani-Sadr tried to gain credibility among radicals by authorizing purges leading to the dismissal of 4,000 civil servants and 4,000 military officers who were considered supporters of the Shah's regime. A renewed wave of executions was embarked upon.

Iranian students raise their fists as they set fire to the U.S. flag, soon after the occupation of the U.S. Embassy in Tehran.

The wreckage of a helicopter used in the abortive U.S. rescue attempt to free the hostages.

The Gulf War

In this confused environment, on September 22, 1980, Iraq invaded Iran. Saddam Hussein, Iraq's president, hoped to emerge as leader of the pan-Arab world by securing territorial concessions from a suppliant Iran and by destroying a troublesome revolution that threatened Iraq and other conservative Arab governments. The Iraqi president believed he could defeat Iran in a few weeks.

His plan, allegedly with American support, was to liberate southern Iran, install Shahpour Bakhtiar and General Oveysi in charge of a "Free Republic of Iran," drawing disaffected Iranians to their banner. Rather than achieving this, however, Hussein strengthened the Iranian revolution and started a war with potentially dangerous repercussions for governments throughout the Middle East.

Two Iranian soldiers run for cover as Iraqi aircraft strafe the area near a bridge, just inside the Iranian border.

The outbreak of hostilities gave Bani-Sadr—Commander in Chief of the Armed Forces—some respite as he assisted in rebuilding Iran's shattered defenses and its leaderless armed forces. In late October, President Carter's emissary made contact with Ayatollah Beheshti and the hostages were finally released in January 1981, too late to help Carter in his reelection bid.

President Bani-Sadr visits a warfront in southern Iran.

In the first six months of the war, Iraq won easy victories and captured over 5,000 square miles of Iranian territory. With the war going badly and without a political base, Bani-Sadr threw in his lot with the Mujahedeen, against his perennial enemies—the radical ulema of the IRP. Bani-Sadr believed that the army would support him in a crisis and the alliance with the Mujahedeen would provide the means to defend himself politically. As it turned out, the IRP moved

faster. Exploiting their majority in the majlis, the IRP removed Bani-Sadr from office on June 20, 1981, a move immediately ratified by Khomeini.

The Mujahedeen challenge
However, with Bani-Sadr's removal came the most serious threat to the regime yet. Since the Mujahedeen had irretrievably lost in the political arena, they decided to mount

Clouds of tear gas waft over members of the Mujahadeen, trapped inside a stadium when their rally was attacked by Muslim militants.

an armed guerrilla campaign using their 10,000 members in Greater Tehran. The *Pasdaran-e-Inqilab-e Islami* (Revolutionary Guard) were established in June 1979 to safeguard the revolution's objectives and to act as a counterweight to the regular army. A year later, the Revolutionary Guard were thrown into urban battle against the Mujahedeen— aiming for their total destruction.

On June 28, a bomb blast at the IRP headquarters where 90 party leaders were meeting in secret session killed 72 people, including Beheshti, 4 cabinet ministers, 10 deputy ministers and 27 majlis deputies. While monarchists in Paris claimed responsibility, the government blamed the Mujahedeen. In the July presidential election, ex-Prime Minister Rajai took most of the votes despite efforts by the Mujahedeen to disrupt the process. On July 28, Bani-Sadr, by now the most wanted man in Iran, fled to asylum in France.

On August 30, the Mujahedeen struck yet again. A bomb placed at a government meeting killed both President Rajai, and the newly appointed prime minister. In elections to fill the presidential vacancy, Khomeini waived his ban on mullahs' contesting, leading to Iran's first clerical president, Ayatollah Khamenei. By early February 1982, the Mujahedeen had killed 1,200 religious and political leaders. The government countered by executing 4,000 Mujahedeen guerrillas, including ten members of the Central Committee, effectively destroying the movement.

On the Iraqi warfront, the Iranian armed forces counterattacked in human waves believing their martyrdom would secure them a place in heaven. Their fierce zeal regained territory from the Iraqis. On May 21, 1981, Iran recaptured the major port of Khorramshahr and continued to make progress, so by the end of the year only 190 square miles of Iranian territory remained in Iraqi hands.

Domestically, the shattered economy was gradually rebuilt. Oil revenues provided $1.5 billion per month, of which military imports accounted for $400 million and civilian imports consumed $700 million. The economy finally grew in 1981–82, reversing a two-year post-revolutionary trend of negative growth.

In April 1982, Sadiq Qotbzadeh, an aide to Khomeini during his Paris exile, who had held various ministerial appointments in post-revolutionary Iran, was implicated in a plot to overthrow the government. Over 170 people, including 70 military officers, were tried, and by September

all, including Qotbzadeh, were executed. A leading liberal mullah implicated in the plot, Ayatollah Shariatmadari, publicly admitted his guilt and was defrocked. True to his belief that violence would not advance Islam, he refused to call on his supporters to revolt, extinguishing any threat from the liberal ulema.

So by the winter of 1982, the Iranian revolution had purged itself of all influences that threatened the primacy of the radical vision of Ayatollah Khomeini.

The burned-out interior of Shariatmadari's party headquarters in Tabriz, attacked by Khomeini's followers.

7
The future

All modern revolutions have ended in a reinforcement of the power of the state.

Albert Camus

In its brief and turbulent history, the Islamic republic has survived a series of challenges that would have defeated most established governments—among them, a debilitating war with Iraq, a year-long American economic boycott prompted by the taking of the hostages at the U.S. Embassy, the loss of trained manpower through purges and emigration and opposition-sponsored terrorism that eliminated the political leadership.

While successfully overcoming these threats, the government used each opportunity to strengthen its rule. Khomeini provided the leadership necessary to encourage the newly formed government and to steer it through its dangerous early days.

Khomeini's successor

Although the Islamic state has survived its perilous infancy, questions remain about its future shape, role and policies. To avoid a dangerously divisive power struggle on Khomeini's death, the 82-member Council of Experts nominated (in November 1985) a favorite student of his as his successor—the 63-year-old Ayatollah Husein Ali Montazeri.

Although Montazeri does not have Khomeini's preeminent revolutionary status, working alongside Khomeini has provided him with an opportunity to establish his primacy among his fellow ulema and the country at large. Montazeri has established his standing as a radical in favor of revolutionary groups and egalitarian policies, and he is said to be flexible with a balanced approach and a greater inclination toward compromise than Ayatollah Khomeini. He will have to assist the government to address a number of contentious issues.

Opposite *Militant Iranian students meet Khomeini to discuss the U.S. hostages.*

Ayatollah Montazeri, the possible successor to Khomeini.

The role of the state in the economy

Khomeini and the economically conservative Council of Guardians have twice vetoed legislation to nationalize trade, and have opposed land reform. Like Khomeini, Montazeri favors a mixed economy with a balanced free enterprise sector. However, a large radical body in the majlis will continue to push for greater government involvement.

The war with Iraq

The Gulf War has now dragged on for more than six years and has claimed one million lives (Iranian casualties number 750,000). Despite Iraq's better equipment and financial support provided by Saudi Arabia and the Gulf States (of about $25 billion), Iran has made of the war a holy crusade, using the revolutionary zeal of its people (Iran has three times the population of Iraq) to great advantage. Not only has Iran recaptured all territory taken by Iraq but has also launched a series of successful attacks into Iraqi territory. Although Iraq has repeatedly sought for peace, Khomeini has called for the overthrow of the Iraqi president, Saddam Hussein, as a precondition for negotiations, as well as massive ($150 billion) war reparations, and the return to Iraq of 100,000 Iraqi Shiites who Saddam Hussein had expelled at the start of the war.

Iran estimates that its war damage up until 1983 was $135.8 billion, which included loss of oil revenues, agricultural output, the destruction of six cities and 1,200 villages, damage to the economy and the creation of 1.5 million refugees. Economically, the war has bankrupted Iraq. At the start of the war, Iraq had $30 billion in reserves; it is now $40 billion in debt, and in 1986 began discussions on debt rescheduling with its creditors.

Although Iran has repaid its external debts incurred under the Shah's regime, and has gradually shifted the war burden to the voluntary sector, the economic burden is becoming very heavy. At current levels Iran's 1986 oil revenues will be $8.4 billion, compared with $14.8 billion for 1985. As the war effort consumed 30 percent of the 1985 budget there will be a significant shortfall in 1986. Iran will probably try to end the war by moving it into a higher gear; if that tactic does not succeed, Iran will probably revert to an extended war of attrition that they can better afford than Iraq. A decisive Iranian victory could change the complexion of Middle East politics, placing conservative Arab

Opposite *The war with Iraq drags on, with no end in sight.*

governments on the defensive.

Foreign policy
An ambitious foreign policy with the slogan "neither East nor West" underpins Iran's international relationships. Iran's antipathy to both the United States and the Soviet Union is deep-rooted. The U.S. is seen as the power that overthrew the Mossadegh government and supported the oppressive regime of the Shah, and that also promotes Israeli ambitions in the Middle East and is a threat to genuine nationalist movements in the Islamic world. The Soviet Union is viewed by its Iranian neighbor as a godless, communist nation crushing the religious aspirations of its 45 million Muslims in the southern republics (there are now 500 mosques in the Soviet Union compared with 25,000 prior to the Bolshevik revolution). It also helps Iraq in the conduct of the war, and has sought to destroy a Muslim revivalist movement by invading Afghanistan.

The war has created more than 1.5 million refugees, like these children in their makeshift classroom.

Conclusion

The religious leaders will probably continue to play a key role in Iranian government unless the war-ravaged economy deteriorates very considerably. Not only do the ulema control both the political and administrative machinery of

A woman mourns at her husband's grave. The Koran says, "God loves those who kill for his way."

*Ayatollah Khamenei,
the first religious leader
to be elected president,
leads prayers in the
battlefield.*

government but the mosques also provide them with a powerful network to reach out to the masses. The only other credible alternative rests with the military. As Napoleon burst forth in post-revolutionary France on a wave of patriotic French victories, several battle-scarred commanders on the Iraqi front may dream they can do likewise. However, such a scene is difficult to envisage as the Iranian armed forces are not a single unit under a unified command but a series of independent and rival bodies made up of a 250,000-man standing army, a navy and air force (of 20,000 and 25,000 respectively), balanced by the 250,000-strong *Pasdaran* (Islamic Guard) who have their own command structure. There are also 2.5 million paramilitary reserve forces. It has been suggested that the Iranian government is quite satisfied to see the continuation of the Gulf War, as this keeps the armed forces occupied away from the political arena, while it consolidates its hold on the country.

The monarchists do not pose a threat to the government as they lack popular support. However, many supporters of the monarchy still harbor hopes that the Shah's family might one day be reinstated.

While the Mujahedeen were successful in inflicting heavy losses on the fledgling government in 1981–82, the organization has been crushed and now lacks mass appeal. Although they may continue to plague the government, their efforts will probably have little effect. The Tudeh Party and the communists lost credibility after the invasion of Afghanistan by the Soviet Union. While it is extremely unlikely that Iranian communists could mount an effective challenge for power, Iran's 1,600-mile common border with the Soviet Union does mean that they could readily exploit a turbulent post-Khomeini period.

Despite its difficulties, the pan-Islamic appeal of the revolutionary government retains general support while mass indoctrination continues. However, the long-term success of the government will depend on how effectively the religious leaders can broaden their vision of an Islamic state to include a more liberal and balanced approach, although still rooted in religious beliefs. If they can successfully adapt, they may be able to establish a middle ground between the superpowers. If, however, they insist on continuing with their narrow, austere vision of a religious state, their broader experiment to provide an alternative model of government will be stillborn.

Glossary

Ayatollah   Sign of God. Title given to religious men of supreme learning and authority at the pinnacle of the Shiite hierarchy. Currently there are six Grand Ayatollahs and twelve Ayatollahs.

Bazaar   Traditional marketplace.

Bazaaris   Merchants.

Caliph   Spiritual and temporal ruler of Muslims.

Fedayeen-e-Khalq   Self-sacrificing guerrillas—a left-wing group aligned with the Communist Party of Iran.

Fetwa   Ruling or decree.

Khan   Honorific meaning chief or leader.

Majlis   Parliament (meeting).

Muharram   The first month in the Muslim calendar.

Mujahedeen-e-Khalq   A major opposition group, literally "peoples' combatants."

Mullah   Muslim scholar, teacher or religious leader. Also title of respect.

National Front   Opposition parties with a social democratic agenda. Mossadegh's party.

Oil nationalization   State purchase of the oil industry.

SAVAK   *Sazemane Etalaat va Amniyat e Keshvar*—Organization for Information and Peace in State—security agency of Iran under the Shah.

Shah   King. Iranian kings were called Shah-in-Shah, or king of kings, as they had sovereignty over the four kings of Afghanistan, Georgia, Kurdistan and Arabistan (now Khuzestan).

Shariah   Law of Islam.

Shiite(s)   Literally partisan(s)—derived from Shiah-e-Ali —partisans of Ali.

Tudeh   Masses—name given to the Communist Party of Iran.

Ulema   Religious leaders in the mosque.

Waqf(s)   Pious endowment(s).

Chronology

622	Prophet Mohammad announces Islam.
632	Prophet Mohammad dies.
650	Hazrat Ali becomes Caliph.
655	Hazrat Ali assassinated.
680	Martyrdom of Imam Husain at Kerbala.
1501	Safavid dynasty introduces Shiism in Iran.
1905–06	Constitutional revolution. Iran becomes constitutional monarchy.
1909	Constitutionalists defeat royalists.
1921	Reza Khan's *coup d'etat* overthrows Qajars.
1926	Reza Khan crowns himself Reza Shah Pahlavi.
1941	Mohammad Reza Pahlavi accedes to throne on abdication of his father.
1951	Bill to nationalize oil passed. Mossadegh becomes prime minister.
1953	CIA-organized *coup d'etat* results in overthrow of Mossadegh.
1962	The "White Revolution."
1963	Anti-government riots led by Khomeini and other religious leaders.
1964	Khomeini exiled to Iraq.
May 1977	Open letter from 53 lawyers calling for free and open judiciary.
July 1977	Prime Minister Hoveiyda replaced by Jamshid Amouzegar.
November 1977	Shah visits President Carter in Washington D.C. Tear gas used to disperse demonstrators.
January 1978	Article published in *Eta'laat* slandering Khomeini leads to demonstrations in religious city of Qom.
February 1978	Demonstrations in Tabriz protesting closing down of mosques.

March 30, 1978	Day of Mourning—demonstrations in 55 cities.
May 10, 1978	Demonstrations in Qom.
May 11, 1978	Demonstrations in Tehran.
June 17, 1978	Shariatmadari calls for general strike in Qom.
August 17, 1978	Local religious leaders arrested in Isfahan after 18 hours of rioting.
August 19, 1978	400 people burned alive in Rex Cinema in Tehran.
August 27, 1978	Resignation of Jamshid Amouzegar government. Jafar Sherif Emami made prime minister with mandate to make concessions to religious opposition.
September 6, 1978	Government announces ban on demonstrations.
September 7, 1978	Half a million people march carrying slogans calling for Khomeini's return and an end to Pahlavi rule. Government announces martial law to begin 6 a.m. September 8.
September 8, 1978	(Black Friday) Jaleh Square massacre —thousands killed.
October 6, 1978	Khomeini expelled from Iraq—flies to Paris.
October 18, 1978	Oil workers strike.
November 5, 1978	Students attack Western banks, airline offices, hotels and the British Embassy.
November 6, 1978	Sherif Emami dismissed and replaced by Armed Forces Chief of Staff.
December 1, 1978	Army declares curfew—people defy curfew and hundreds killed.
December 11, 1978	2 million people demonstrate in Tehran.
December 29, 1978	Shahpour Bakhtiar appointed prime minister.
January 15, 1979	Parliament accepts Bakhtiar's government.
January 16, 1979	Shah leaves country.
January 19, 1979	Khomeini calls for demonstrations against Bakhtiar. 1 million march in Tehran.

January 26, 1979	Khomeini plans to come to Tehran but Bakhtiar closes airport.
February 1, 1979	Khomeini returns.
February 9, 1979	Radicals attack military bases.
February 12, 1979	Victory of the revolution.
April 1, 1979	Establishment of Islamic republic.
October 23, 1979	Shah enters the United States on medical grounds.
November 4, 1979	U.S. Embassy in Tehran overrun and 52 hostages taken.
January 1980	Bani-Sadr elected president.
March–May 1980	First parliamentary elections result in majority for Islamic Republic Party.
April 25, 1980	The United States launches abortive military strike to free hostages.
September 22, 1980	Iraq invades Iran.
January 20, 1981	Bani-Sadr removed from presidency.
June 28, 1981	Bomb blast kills 72 leading political figures.
August 30, 1981	Bomb kills President Rajai and newly elected Prime Minister Bahonar.

Index

Picture acknowledgments

The publishers would like to thank the following for allowing their photographs to be reproduced in this book: BBC Hulton Picture Library 13, 21; Camera Press Ltd *cover*; Popperfoto 8, 9, 14, 15, 16, 17, 20, 23, 24, 26, 27, 28, 29, 30, 31, 34, 35, 36, 37, 38, 40, 42, 43, 44, 47, 50, 42, 54, 58, 61, 65, 68; Topham *frontispiece*, 11, 19, 22, 25, 32, 33, 46, 48, 53, 56, 57, 63, 64, 66, 67, 71; Malcolm S. Walker 10, 12.